To Kendra, my
Irish Buddy

THE
IRISH

from Dottie
3-17-94

THE
IRISH

A Tribute to the Emerald Isle

Ariel Books
Andrews and McMeel
Kansas City

ISBN: 0–8362–3031–0

Library of Congress Catalog Number: 92–73435

THE
IRISH

THE IRISH

O Ireland, isn't it grand you look—
Like a bride in her rich adornin'?
And with all the pent-up love of my heart
I bid you the top o' the mornin'!

JOHN LOCKE,
The Exile's Return

IRELAND

A RICH HISTORY

Ireland is only about the size of West Virginia. Wherever you happen to stop for a pint, you'll never be farther than 70 miles from the sea, and yet this tiny island land has one of the richest histories in the Western world.

IMPORTANT DATES

c. 600 B.C. ♣ Celtic tribes arrive on Irish soil.

c. A.D. 432 ♣ St. Patrick brings Christianity to Ireland.

500–800 ♣ The Golden Age of Ireland, a period of great artistic and literary creativity that made Irish scholars the most revered in Europe.

c. 800 ♣ The Vikings invade Ireland and subsequently found the first towns, including the city of Dublin in 988.

1002 ♣ Brian, of the kingdom of Dal Cais in west Munster, unites Ireland for the first time under one leader.

THE IRISH

1171 ♣ The Normans, under Henry II, conquer Ireland, beginning 750 years of British domination.

1609 ♣ Protestantism takes root in Northern Ireland after British Protestant forces defeat native Irish Catholics in a bloody nine-year war.

1801 ♣ Ireland is made part of the United Kingdom.

1845 ♣ A million and a half Irish starve to death during the Great Potato Famine, and a million more emigrate to avoid a similar fate.

1916 ♣ The Irish Republican Army stages the Easter Rebellion to protest British conscription of Irishmen for their military forces in WWI. The rebellion is crushed, and its leaders are martyred.

1922 ♣ Ireland becomes a Free State within the British Commonwealth, except for the six Ulster counties of Northern Ireland, which remain part of the United Kingdom.

1949 ♣ The twenty-six counties of Ireland become an independent republic.

IRELAND'S NATURAL SPLENDOR

CLIMATE

The Emerald Isle gets its name from its rolling green countryside, kept verdant by the almost daily rain. Lush landscapes are not all the rain brings; there's also the magic of a rainbow every day!

THE IRISH

Your wits can't thicken in that soft moist air, on those white springy roads, in those misty rushes and brown bogs, on those hillsides of granite rocks and magenta heather. You've no such colours in the sky, no such lure in the distance, no such sadness in the evenings. Oh the dreaming! the dreaming! the torturing, heart scalding, never satisfying dreaming, dreaming, dreaming.

GEORGE BERNARD SHAW,
John Bull's Other Island

God made the grass, the air and the rain; and the grass, the air and the rain made the Irish; and the Irish turned the grass, the air and the rain back into God.

SEAN O'FAOLAIN

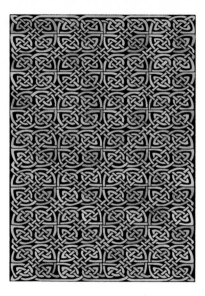

GEOGRAPHY

Ireland is made up of four provinces, Ulster, Connacht, Leinster, and Munster, which are divided into thirty-two counties. Six counties in the province of Ulster make up the territory of Northern Ireland.

PROVINCE
OF CONNACHT

Galway	Roscommon
Leitrim	Sligo
Mayo	

PROVINCE OF MUNSTER

Clare	Kerry	Tipperary
Cork	Limerick	Waterford

THE IRISH

PROVINCE OF LEINSTER

Carlow	Leix (Laois)	Offaly
Dublin	Longford	Westmeath
Kildare	Louth	Wexford
Kilkenny	Meath	Wicklow

PROVINCE OF ULSTER
(Republic of Ireland)

Cavan	Donegal	Monaghan

(Northern Ireland)

Antrim	Derry/Londonderry	Fermanagh
Armagh	Down	Tyrone

SYMBOLS
OF IRELAND

ST. PATRICK

t. Patrick, the man who converted the Irish to Christianity, is the most famous Irishman of all time. The Irish are not sure where their patron saint was born or where he is buried, but they all know the day he died, March 17. On that day, the Irish worldwide celebrate the holiday named in his honor.

THE HARP

The harp, of the small portable type played by Celtic minstrels, is the oldest official symbol of Ireland. Though not as recognizable as the shamrock, the harp is widely used. It appears on Irish coins, the presidential flag, state seals, uniforms, and official documents. But the harp is most often associated with Guinness, which adopted the harp as its trademark in 1862.

THE SHAMROCK

The shamrock is undoubtedly the most identifiable symbol of Ireland. *Shamrock* comes from the Gaelic *Seamrog*, a word that refers to the plant's three leaves. Legend has it that during a religious debate with the Druid priests, St. Patrick plucked a shamrock to demonstrate the mysteries of the Christian Trinity—three leaves held together by a single stem. Whether or not this story is true, the shamrock is regarded as the national plant of Ireland and always worn on St. Patrick's Day.

THE IRISH FLAG

The Irish tricolor made its debut in 1848. It was based on the French tricolor; however, the colors were altogether Irish. One outside band was made green, the color that had long been used as the symbol of the Catholic majority. The other outside band, a stripe of orange, was chosen to represent the Protestant minority. And the middle band of white represented their unity.

IRISH FOLKLORE

FAIRIES
AND SPIRITS

For centuries Irish legends have spoken about mystical creatures that inhabit the earth, known as the *Sidhe*, or spirit race, or the *Feadh-Ree*, from which we get the word *fairy*. These creatures are said to be halfway between angels and humans. They once dwelt in heaven but were expelled as punishment for their pride. Some fell onto Irish soil and and some into the Irish Sea, where they became "merrows"—water fairies and merpeople.

THE IRISH

FAIRIES

The fairies inhabit a country called *Tir-na-hog*, the Gaelic mythical land of eternal youth, but they are found living in the bushes and circles of stones that crop up all over Ireland—the fairy raths. The fairies are said to be very beautiful, with long yellow hair and perfect delicate forms. They love milk and honey and drink flower nectar as their fairy wine. The fairies can assume any form and can make horses out of straw. They have the power to affect human life, especially unbaptized children. The fairies also love music, often luring mortals into an eternal dance with their piping and singing.

THE IRISH

The land of faery,
Where nobody gets old and godly and grave,
Where nobody gets old and crafty and wise,
Where nobody gets old and bitter of tongue.

W. B. YEATS,
The Land of Heart's Desire

FAIRY RATHS

Rings of stones, called fairy raths or forts, crop up in pastures all over Ireland, and the farmers never plow them up for fear of disturbing the fairies who live there and bringing down some bad luck upon themselves.

BANSHEES

Banshee or *Bean-sidhe* is Irish for "fairy woman." When one of these wailing ghosts raps on the window pane at night, it is a portent of the death of a loved one. Banshees attach themselves only to the best families in Ireland, those with the most ancient Celtic lineages.

LEPRECHAUNS

he little leprechaun is said to possess the secret of how to find hidden gold. With an herb and a chant known only to him, he can uncover buried treasure and find untold wealth.

FLYING POOKA AND WILL-O'-THE-WISPS

 ooka are ghosts that take the shapes of goats, horses, or great dogs, and fly through the air creating a great deal of usually harmless hubbub. On the other hand, will-o'-the-wisps, or fairy lights, are quiet and helpful. They appear in the misty Irish mountains to help searchers to locate someone lost in a ravine or drowned in a rocky pool. It's said that those who can see the lights have the gift of knowing when their closest of kin are in danger.

THE BURREN

The Burren, Irish for "gray rocky place," is 50 square miles of great irregular slabs of limestone with deep cracks. Located in County Clare, this humid, eerie moonscape is a natural rock garden, where plants native to the Arctic thrive next to subtropical flora. Beneath the scarred surface are spectacular caves and streams.

Folk legends associated with the Burren say its holy wells can cure bad vision and its caves are home to ghostly horsemen. It is also reputed that mysterious lakes appear and disappear there, taking with them maidens who have been turned into swans.

THE BLARNEY STONE

 block of limestone known as the Blarney Stone is Ireland's lucky charm. Set in a tower of Blarney Castle in County Cork in 1446, the stone is reputed to have magical powers. Legend has it that an old woman cast a spell on a king as a reward for saving her life. Under this spell, if he kissed the stone he'd gain great powers of eloquence. Today people travel from all over the world to kiss the stone and gain the gift of gab.

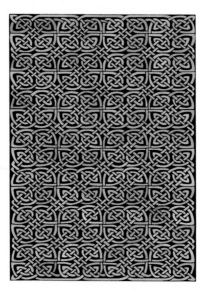

IRISH FOOD
AND DRINK

Only 150 years after the Great Potato Famine in Ireland, the Irish are perhaps the best-fed people in the world, consuming more calories on average than the citizens of any other country.

The Irish not only eat well, they eat frequently. Between morning tea and bedtime, they may consume as many as six meals or snacks.

IRISH FOOD

Irish breakfasts are particularly famous, featuring oatmeal with milk, eggs, rashers of bacon, and fresh bread slathered with butter and jam. Then there is a mid-morning snack of pastry, a prelude to the main meal of dinner. Dinner always features some sort of meat—roast beef, corned beef, steak, ham, or perhaps Irish stew, made with lamb or mutton. And, of course, no dinner would be complete without potatoes, served in as many as four different styles.

The Irish are also expert bakers. There is always a freshly baked loaf on the table at mealtime. The Irish are famous for their soda bread, which is leavened with baking soda instead of yeast, and are also fans of brown bread, made of stone-ground whole wheat. The Irish are also known for their sweet tooth. Plum pudding, trifle, sultana (yellow raisin) cake, and apple tart are among the most popular desserts.

TEA

For each cup of coffee they drink, the Irish consume three to four cups of tea. From breakfast until bedtime, tea is a constant fixture of daily life. Virtually every meal is served with a pot of the strong, sweet brew.

BEER, ALE, AND SPIRITS

he Irish are well known for their apprecia-
tion of good drink. Beer and ale are almost
as important to the Irish diet as food, and
pub life is a critical aspect of Irish social culture.
It is estimated that the average imbiber spends 14
percent of his or her disposable income on drink.

Stout, a strong, dark, malty-tasting beer, is Ireland's most popular drink. And Guinness, a
name that is basically synonymous with stout, is
a national treasure. The Guinness family began
brewing its stout in 1759 along the banks of Dublin's Liffey River, where it has been produced ever

since. Today the Guinness brewery covers one square mile and has its own railroad. Guinness claims over 60 percent of the beer market in Ireland and is exported to more than 100 countries around the world. But the Irish claim that it is best when consumed in its native land, straight from the tap.

Another popular native product is Irish whiskey. There are several brands, each with its own distinctive taste, and people tend to remain loyal to one. In contrast to American or Canadian whiskey, the Irish variety is made with barley, not corn or rye. It is then malted and distilled three times, giving it a smoother, milder flavor than Scotch, which is distilled only once.

PUB CULTURE

n the small villages that dot Ireland, the pub plays an important role in social life; it is the social hub of the community. For instance, Dingle town—population 1,000—boasts more than 50 pubs. That's one pub for every 20 people. Village folks don't sit in front of the tube after supper; they meet at the local pub and don't go home until everyone at the table's politely bought a round.

Shaw maintained that the Irish find their imaginations too tortuous to bear without whiskey. More likely it's the pub as much as the pint that the Irish would find life unbearable without.

When I die I want to decompose in a barrel of porter [dark beer] and have it served in all the pubs of Dublin. I wonder would they know it was me?

J. P. DONLEAVY,
The Ginger Man

THE AMERICAN CONNECTION

From the very beginning, the Irish have played a critical role in the history of the United States.

As many as one-third to one-half of the American troops during the Revolutionary War were of Irish descent. Among them, 1,500 were officers and 26 were generals.

Eight of the men who signed the Declaration of Independence were of Irish descent. The document itself was handwritten by Irish-born Charles Thomson and printed by another Irishman, John Dunlap.

49

THE IRISH

Many of the great American folk heroes were really Irishmen. Among them was Sam Houston, the first president of the Lone Star State, whose family came from Ballynure in County Antrim. Daniel Boone, first to explore Kentucky, was originally Daniel Buhun. Davy Crockett, son of a Londonderry immigrant, became the "King of the Wild Frontier."

Seventeen of America's presidents were of Irish heritage: John Adams, James Monroe, John Quincy Adams, Andrew Jackson, James K. Polk, James Buchanan, Andrew Johnson, Ulysses S. Grant, Chester A. Arthur, Grover Cleveland, Benjamin Harrison, William McKinley, Theodore Roosevelt, Woodrow Wilson, John F. Kennedy, Richard M. Nixon, and Ronald Reagan.

OTHER FAMOUS IRISH-AMERICANS

William F. Buckley ♣ *(journalist)*

James Cagney ♣ *(actor)*

Jimmy Connors ♣ *(tennis player)*

Bing Crosby ♣ *(entertainer)*

Jack Dempsey ♣ *(boxer)*

F. Scott Fitzgerald ♣ *(writer)*

Henry Ford ♣ *(auto maker, industrialist)*

John Ford ♣ *(director)*

Jackie Gleason ♣ *(actor)*

Helen Hayes ♣ *(actress)*

William Randolph Hearst ♣ *(publisher, industrialist)*

Howard Hughes ♣ *(industrialist)*

THE IRISH

Gene Kelly ♣ *(dancer, actor)*

Grace Kelly ♣ *(actress)*

Edward Kennedy ♣ *(senator)*

Robert F. Kennedy ♣ *(attorney general)*

John McEnroe ♣ *(tennis player)*

Margaret Mitchell ♣ *(writer)*

Daniel Moynihan ♣ *(senator)*

Edward R. Murrow ♣ *(journalist)*

Flannery O'Connor ♣ *(writer)*

Sandra Day O'Connor ♣ *(Supreme Court justice)*

Georgia O'Keeffe ♣ *(artist)*

Eugene O'Neill ♣ *(playwright)*

Gregory Peck ♣ *(actor)*

Ed Sullivan ♣ *(television host, entertainer)*

Louis Sullivan ♣ *(architect)*

Spencer Tracy ♣ *(actor)*

IRISH
PROVERBS

I rish proverbs come from two sources—
some are from the ancient Gaelic tradition,
others were brought over by the British.
These maxims embody the wisdom of many gen-
erations concerning life and how it ought to be
lived.

THE IRISH

- ♣ Where the tongue slips, it speaks the truth.
- ♣ What's got badly, goes badly.
- ♣ He who can follow his own will is a king.
- ♣ Pity him who makes his opinion a certainty.
- ♣ A little help is better than a great deal of pity.
- ♣ Unwillingness easily finds an excuse.
- ♣ Forsake not a friend of many years for an acquaintance of a day.
- ♣ Falling is easier than rising.
- ♣ Have sense, patience, and self-restraint, and no mischief will come.
- ♣ A foot at rest meets nothing.
- ♣ True greatness knows gentleness.
- ♣ There is no joy without affliction.

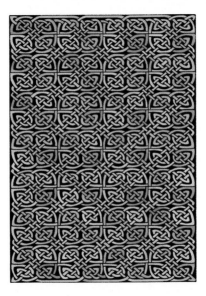

IRISH SONGS

DANNY BOY

Oh Danny Boy, the pipes the pipes are calling,
from glen to glen and down the mountain side.
The summer's gone and all the roses falling,
'tis you 'tis you must go and I must bide.
But come ye back when summer's in the
    meadow,
or when the valley's hushed and white with
    snow.
'Tis there I'll be in the sunshine and shadow.
Oh Danny Boy, oh Danny Boy, I love you so.

THE IRISH

THE WEST'S AWAKE

When all beside a vigil keep,
The West's asleep, The West's asleep.
Alas, and well may Erin weep
That Cannacht lies in slumber deep,
There lake and plain a mile fair and free,
'Mid rocks their guardian chivalry,
Sing, oh! let man learn liberty,
From crashing wind and lashing sea.

THE IRISH

THE PARTING GLASS

Oh, all the money I e'er had,
I spent it in good company,
And all the harm I've ever done,
Alas it was to none but me.
And all I've done for want of wit
To mem'ry now I can't recall;
So fill to me the parting glass,
Good night and joy be with you all.

LITERARY
TRADITION

Ireland has a dual literary heritage of Gaelic and Anglo-Irish literature. Gaelic is an ancient tongue, one of a group of Indo-European languages to which English belongs. It was an oral language until the 8th century, when St. Patrick's Christian monks gave it an alphabet.

Gaelic is usually referred to as Irish by the people, and although most people speak and write in English, Irish is the official first language of Ireland.

THE IRISH

The English language brings out the best in the Irish. They court it like a beautiful woman. They make it bray with donkey laughter. They hurl it at the sky like a paint pot full of rainbows, and then make it chant a dirge for man's fate and man's follies that is as mournful as misty spring rain crying over the fallow earth.

T. E. KALEM

THE IRISH

There is no language like the Irish for soothing and quieting.

JOHN SYNGE

Everywhere in Irish prose there twinkles and peers the merry eye and laugh of a people who had little to laugh about in real life.

DIARMUID RUSSELL

THE GREATEST IRISH WRITERS, POETS, AND PLAYWRIGHTS

JONATHAN SWIFT (1667–1745)
novelist, essayist, satirist
Gulliver's Travels
"A Modest Proposal"

OSCAR WILDE (1854–1900)
novelist, poet, essayist, satirist
The Picture of Dorian Gray
The Importance of Being Earnest

THE IRISH

GEORGE BERNARD SHAW (1856–1950)
playwright, writer
Pygmalion
Arms and the Man
Major Barbara

WILLIAM BUTLER YEATS (1865–1939)
poet
"Leda and the Swan"
"Who Goes with Fergus"
"The Lake Isle of Innisfree"

JAMES JOYCE (1882–1941)
novelist
The Dubliners
Portrait of the Artist as a Young Man
Ulysses

THOUGHTS
ON IRELAND

For the great Gaels of Ireland
Are the men that God made mad,
For all their wars are merry,
And all their songs are sad.

G. K. CHESTERTON

THE IRISH

Land of Heart's Desire,
Where beauty has no ebb, decay no flood,
But joy is wisdom, time an endless song.

WILLIAM BUTLER YEATS

O Ireland my first and only love
Where Christ and Caesar are hand in
    glove.

JAMES JOYCE

Where there are Irish there's loving and fighting
And when we stop either, it's Ireland no more!

RUDYARD KIPLING

THE IRISH

Ireland's ruins are historic emotions surrendered to time.

HORACE SUTTON

The Gael is not like other men; the spade, and the lom, and the sword are not for him. But a destiny more glorious than that of Rome, more glorious than that of Britain, awaits him: to become the savior of idealism in modern intellectual and social life.

PATRICK PEARSE,
Irish novelist

THE IRISH

We have always found the Irish a bit odd. They refuse to be English.

WINSTON CHURCHILL

My one claim to originality among Irishmen is that I have never made a speech.

GEORGE MOORE,
Irish author

THE IRISH

The graceful Georgian streets and squares, a
series of steel engravings under a wet sky.

SHANA ALEXANDER,
"Dublin Is My Sure Thing"

Ah, Ireland . . . that damnable, delightful
country, where everything that is right is the
opposite of what it ought to be.

BENJAMIN DISRAELI,
Earl of Beaconsfield

THE IRISH

I will arise and go now, and go to Innisfree . . .
And live alone in the bee-loud glade.
I hear lake water lapping with low
     sounds by the shore;
While I stand on the roadway, or on the
     pavements grey,
I hear it in the deep heart's core.

WILLIAM BUTLER YEATS,
"The Lake Isle of Innisfree"

ERIN
GO BRAGH—
"IRELAND
FOREVER."

The text of this book was set in Tiffany Lite,
and the display was set in University Roman
by Dix Type Inc., Syracuse, New York.

Celtic art hand colored by Robyn Officer.

Design by Diane Stevenson/
SNAP-HAUS GRAPHICS.